REDESIGNING YOUR LIFE

WHEN YOUR SPOUSE HAS DIED

Marilyn Gustin

One Liguori Drive
Liguori MO 63057-9999

Imprimi Potest:
Richard Thibodeau, C.Ss.R.
Provincial, Denver Province
The Redemptorists

ISBN 0-7648-0798-6
Library of Congress Catalog Card Number:
2001091026

© 2002, Marilyn Gustin
Printed in the United States of America
02 03 04 05 06 5 4 3 2 1

All rights reserved. No part of this booklet may be reproduced, stored in a retrieval system, or transmitted without the written permission of Liguori Publications.

To order, call 1-800-325-9521
www.liguori.org
www.catholicbooksonline.com

If you have picked up this book, you are probably experiencing great pain. Someone you love is no longer with you.

Perhaps that death is recent, perhaps it has been awhile since your loved one died. Perhaps you have been advised, as I was, that you just have to "hang in there and learn to cope."

If so, please know that is not the case. There is a better way, a way of living with your new situation positively, constructively, a way to face your pain even while you help it to diminish as fast as possible. In fact, there is a way to put your pain to good use, so that you can redesign your life to fit your new circumstances. I offer you my experience and reflections to help you know that, even though death is extraordinarily difficult, it also offers a precious opportunity—to redesign your life.

> *Even though death is extraordinarily difficult, it also offers a precious opportunity.*

Here is how the most painful period of my life—and, as it turned out, the most adventuresome and profoundly rewarding—began.

As I opened the door to our home, my beloved husband, John, got up from his chair to meet me with a kiss and a hug—the sweet welcome that was always there for me when I'd been out. In his arms, I told him about the evening meeting I'd been to. He laughed at part of my tale. Then he felt pain, laid down on the floor, and as I held his hand in one of mine and the phone in the other, his heart stopped. He was gone from this world. And though I certainly wasn't thinking about the implications in the shock of that moment, the splendid, shared life of love and joy that we had both cherished was over. In three minutes, with no warning, it was over.

That is, the shared part was over, or so I experienced it almost all the time. The love was not over, nor the joy, nor the splendor of life. But the night he died, I had yet to discover all that.

Of course, I had no idea that evening

what this utterly unwelcome change would mean to me. I knew only horrific shock. I focused on what I had to do next—make phone calls, visit the mortuary, plan the funeral Mass, greet family and friends. I didn't want any of it. As you too may have done for those first days, I only put one foot in front of the other, alternately doing necessary things, responding to the love of dear ones, and weeping and thinking and—well, you know!

Then something happened that I never could have predicted. It changed the course of my grief—and my life. It turned my attention to a new possibility.

A few days after John died, I was out walking. The desert dawn was lovely as always, and I'd always delighted in these morning hours. But I was still feeling stunned and filled with sadness. I watched the birds and bunnies as I went. I talked, sometimes out loud, to God, as if I were thinking aloud with the Lord. I hurt. All of me seemed to hurt. As I turned my steps toward home, the unexpected happened. Without any preliminary, a mighty shock of joy pierced my whole being, like a lightning bolt, only it came from inside me. Joy blazed within me, dynamic and free, so enormous, so all-consuming that I could find no other feeling. My joy-filled heart lifted my body, and I danced in the street all the way home—a little glad that it was too early for most of the neighbors! This joy-shock was almost as overwhelming as the shock of John's death.

At the time, I thought this experience was a phenomenal gift for me. And it was. But as I lived with it, I came to believe it was not for me alone but for all others whose spouse or other loved ones have died. It was for all those who don't want to wallow in the sorrow and bewilderment of the death of a loved one. It was perhaps even more for you than for me.

Our society defines a post-death experience as loss. People say, "You lost your spouse." We are expected to find comfort in memories and the love of family and friends, if we find any at all. We tend to view our experience as if it is only a collection of miseries that we have to get through somehow. In my experience, all those elements were there, as I think they are for everyone. But the months since John's death have taught me that there is much, much more. My own experience has convinced me that pain, though difficult beyond words, need not be everything for any of us whose beloved has gone to another life.

In fact, we, too, have gone to another life, even though it is one we did not choose and maybe—like me—didn't even expect. In the beginning, it is a new life we'd definitely prefer not to have. To this day, over two years later as I write, I would be excited and thrilled beyond expression if I could share even an hour with my husband John. At the very same time, as I reflect over

> *There was the grief. And there was the awareness of the opportunity to redesign my life, to align it more and more with my highest and dearest ideals.*

those two-plus years, I know that they also have brought great gifts, gifts that I probably would not have accepted were John still here.

As I lived from one day to the next, it was as if two streams of experience were running side by side within me. There was the grief—not to be denied or wished away. And there was the awareness of opportunity—the opportunity to redesign my life, to align it more and more with my highest and dearest ideals. This booklet describes my experience with this way of responding to the death of a loved one. I offer it to you, because I know that if you wish, you, too, can discover a way of living that takes you beyond the pain of your grief into a new and wonderful life.

Along the way, I realized that much of what I was guided to do, much of what I was shown about this process, could be expressed in simple principles. You will find these principles for action printed in special boxes so you can locate them easily.

This offering is necessarily an intensely personal writing. Your actual experience will be different, tailored to you, with nuances and specific actions all your own. I believe that these principles will hold, however. If you say, "But I didn't experience it that way," please hold firmly to your own experience. Then look to the principle and experiment with it, to find out for yourself if the principle is helpful for you. The results of my experience are hardly the last word! You may also find principles of your own as you live along this new path. Trust them. They are God's gift of new understanding, which God offers to your heart.

You are welcome to come along on my learning journey. Let's begin at the beginning—that single moment when, for me, life entered a new dimension.

I confess that I did not remember God in the moments of John's dying. I would like to say that I turned immediately to God in prayer. I didn't. I was in a state of focused panic, part of me knowing he was gone, part of me trying to do CPR at the direction of the 911 dispatcher. After the final emergency-room details, I was focused on getting through the first necessities, those details that feel like the hardest things we have ever done. I called John's daughters around midnight, greeted them as they arrived, and sipped water to prevent desert dehydration, hoping I would not throw up. I lay down about 3:30 a.m. but didn't sleep.

> *You are welcome to come along on my learning journey.*

Only the next day did I really remember that God was in this, too. As I remembered God—who was after all my first love—I came to know that I must let God be my companion and guide through this awful experience. Though I didn't recognize it then, this was the first of many principles that I would learn. I needed, no matter what, to take time each day to pray, to stay with my spiritual reading, and to practice contemplation. These were already—and still are—staples of my daily life. Thank God, the Spirit let me know that I must not stop doing them, no matter how I felt. And a dear friend reminded me when I needed it.

I can't say that I always wanted to do these practices. I can't say, as many people can, that prayer always made me feel better. Many times it would have been easier to distract myself altogether. It was only after a few

> *I must let God be my companion and guide through this.*

weeks that I realized what a profound support God was through these daily spiritual practices.

As the days passed, I began to internalize several important realizations. The first and hardest was that our loving, joy-filled marriage was past, gone. It would, in time, become a memory only. It was by far the most painful fact I've ever had to accept. But death is implacable—there's no changing it and no imagining it to be otherwise. It is difficult beyond describing, as you probably know too well. But it is also clean: it will not change. We must face it. We can't pretend death away. John would not come out of the next room to hug me. Not today. Not ever.

I also realized that grief was going to be hard and long. People told me I would hurt this much for at least a year. I've never liked pain, so the prospect of a long grieving was not appealing, to say the least. The truth is, the very notion of hurting for so long aroused a huge rebellion in me. I wanted it all to stop hurting right now!

Then came that morning walk, with its

joy-shock, as I've come to think of it. The joy stayed with me for a few hours. I was in wonder. How could this be? What did it mean? Why was it even in me?

I began to know that what the saints say is true: there is within us a joy that is available to us *no matter what the circumstances,* if we only allow our hearts to be open. And in grieving, as in many other painful experiences, hearts break open. The joy deep inside us can be covered over, hidden, by lots of life experiences—pain, distraction, desire, focus on externals, and many other aspects of living. Yet this joy flows constantly inside, because it is God's Presence. God wants us to experience its reality throughout every other experience.

As hours went by, the intensity of joy diminished. I simply could not hold it. But it revealed God's presence to me and showed me my next step.

I saw that I now had a choice. It wasn't a choice I wanted, but it stood unavoidably before me: I could focus backward and keep on wishing things were as they had been for so many years; I could put my missing John at the center of my life and spend my days in perpetual mourning; I could try to make memories my mainstay.

Or I could take seriously God's joyful presence; I could look forward, toward life as it now would be—without my best and dearest friend, but with God, and maybe even in a deeper relationship with God.

If I lived in the past, centered on memories that both comforted and hurt me, I could see that pain would last longer. Wishing for something impossible is not conducive to happy living! Or, while facing the pain and giving grief its due, I could be proactive and, with God's help, change my life. I could move deliberately toward a future that, though yet unknown, could be a full expression of my own self. I could rediscover spontaneous delight in living. I knew without question what my husband would want me to choose: he would want me to be grateful for what was, to remember him with love, and to move forward happily as I created a beautiful way of life—a new life of my own.

And so, facing this choice, I learned that death presents us with an opportunity to redesign our life, to begin again, and to make of our future what we most truly want it to become. This opportunity is before us whether we want it or not, whether we recognize it or not. Many people stumble into their necessarily new lifestyle—life without their spouse. Looking back after years, they realize that though it's been hard, much good has occurred. I didn't want to stumble into anything. And I didn't want to wait for years to understand what was happening or to enjoy some fruits of this new opportunity. I believed that redesigning my life consciously and with purpose would be much better.

> *Death presents us with an opportunity to redesign our life.*

And so it has been. This journey into a new way of being has been the most adventuresome and joyful of my whole life, even though it also gave me some of the most intense pain I have ever known. I would not have expected it to be either adventuresome or joyful. Those qualities have appeared in the redesigning, as if to make clear that life is not ever meant to stagnate, no matter what has happened.

So how do we take this opportunity to redesign? How can we begin?

The first thing I had to do was say yes to the future. Without God, I don't think I could have done this, certainly not for many, many months. It was a future I didn't want in the beginning. I wanted the past! But with my heart turned toward the Lord, I had to take my life in hand with caring attention. As I accepted the choice between past and future, as I said yes to the future, I tried to re-frame the way I experienced John's aching absence. My prayer became

> *Please, Beloved Lord, turn all my longing for John into longing for you alone; turn all my love for John into love for you alone; and please don't let me waste any of this experience. When I must weep, let it be clean crying until the emotion lets up. Then return my attention to your love. Keep my heart open. I accept. Just please, God, stand by!*

Once I'd said that yes and begun to pray that prayer, I turned to the dozens of cards that had arrived after John's death. It was wonderful that so many people cared about me and about John. I acknowledged with gratitude and prayer their support. Now, with a new sense of direction, I looked at the content of these cards.

One repeated theme appeared—learning to cope. Cope? How I resisted that notion! "Coping" reminded me of that old poster of a cat hanging from a branch by its toenails. That I decidedly did not want to do! Nor did I want to crawl miserably through each day. I wanted to live. I wanted meaning. I wanted fulfilled living, even though I didn't yet see how that could be. I also didn't want to wait one day longer than necessary for the awful pain to be gone.

> *The first thing I had to do was say yes to the future.*

Oh, people of faith! Let's not cope! Let's look life straight in the face, accept what has to be accepted, and say yes to the future God will help us build. An affirming attitude will give God space to act in us and create with us a truly beautiful way of living. Let's encourage each other to take heart and do more—much more—than cope. (Coping may be all right for a few weeks, but it's a lousy lifestyle.)

Other cards suggested that I look backward and sit in the not-so-comfortable comfort of memories. I had already said no to that as a predominant attitude. Today—many months later—memories are finally comforting. But they were not in the beginning! Your experience may be different, but I believe God turned my desire away from memories that burned, so that I could see the larger opportunity.

The card that meant the most to me, that for months sat on my dining table before me at every meal, said, "My barn having burned to the ground, I can now see the moon." Precisely. Saying yes to the future God held open to me meant that I wanted to focus on that higher possibility. I didn't want to lose any more time than necessary wailing over the charred barn timbers, the emptiness where the barn had stood.

Not that I didn't wail! I did, a lot. I paced around home, hugging John's picture to my chest, crying, "It's all gone, Johnny, it's all gone!" I woke up in the night, trembling from head to foot, sometimes for half an hour, and then the flood would come, and I'd weep myself back to sleep. Crying spells would come upon me in the most unexpected places—like the produce department of the grocery store. This is normal grief processing. I did not expect it to be any different for me than for anyone. So I didn't fight those excruciating hours but let them sweep over me as fully as possible.

This crying is necessary. It is good. Don't try to avoid it! That's one of the principles of redesigning. Let this grief flow. It hurts, but it helps, too. If it doesn't flow *through* you, it will clog up your emotional life. It will make redesigning very, very difficult. If a spell catches you at a time you find inappropriate—for me it was the produce department—hang on until you get to your car or your home. Then get back in touch with those feelings and let them roll over you like giant waves. Crying will not drown you. Like waves, it will carry you to a new place inside—a gentler place.

In the inner quiet that follows emotional release, I could start to assess my life, with an eye toward the new, unknown design. In the beginning, I had no idea what I wanted my life to be like. I didn't know what I wanted it to become. I had to give myself time and opportunity to find out what I had,

> *This crying is necessary. It is good. Don't try to avoid it!*

what I liked, what I wanted. I needed to look at my daily activities, at the things I had enjoyed. I needed to see what I would want to keep and what I'd want to let go, now that my partner was not at my side.

I found I could not do this assessment by sitting and thinking. It seemed I knew so little. I did know that I loved God, and I wanted that relationship to continue and deepen. Some of the activities John and I loved together I had enjoyed before I married him, but now—now what would they feel like?

Gradually, I saw that I wasn't totally bereft. But still I couldn't define the meaning of my life now. I had centered so much of my activity and so many of my choices on our shared life, which we had enjoyed so thoroughly. That centeredness and all it implied seemed now to be gone or called into question. I had no idea what I would now do when I wasn't at work.

Real progress in redesigning my life began with a life assessment. And so I learned that a life assessment is a good place to begin redesigning. We have to know where we are before we can map our way to a new place. When we see clearly at least some of what has gone and some of what we still have and still *are,* we recognize where we can begin. It is necessary to start where we are.

For me that meant taking a careful, clear look at what my life still included, even though John was gone. I found that I had a place to live. I had family and lots of good friends, including friends who were "my" friends more than "our" friends. I had my work as a craniosacral therapist and personal consultant, work that was part of my earning power and that wasn't dependent on John. I had a spiritual life that was protective and nourishing. I still liked to do

> *A life assessment is a good place to begin redesigning.*

many of the things that John and I had enjoyed together—music and the performing arts, hiking, picnics. I also had my own hobbies and interests, activities that John had supported but that I certainly could enjoy without him.

These aspects of life, already in place, became parts of my new design. You will have your own list of what is still present to you, still living in you. These activities, likes, and enjoyments will become part of your newly designed life, too. And in the meantime, they help you know that *you* are present for *yourself* in spite of the huge change that has occurred.

Because of my background in a healing profession, I've long understood that in hard times the body needs special attention. I knew that the emotions that I was now experiencing were putting pressure on my body. So I resolved to do the healthy things. And I did them whether I felt like doing them or not. I ate well, I rested a lot, I got massages, I worked, I shared, I prayed and meditated, I walked.

> *It's important to do the healthy things whether we feel like doing them or not.*

It is necessary to take care of our body. All too many people have become physically ill after the death of a partner, and I experienced the reason: there was part of me that didn't want to take care of myself.

At first, food was a nuisance and mealtimes were hard alone at the table (so I put cherished pictures, poems, and sayings there to help). Other self-care activities were uninteresting. I did them anyway.

We must also exercise. The body is designed to move. It will get weak if we don't take care of it by moving it around. But we feel sooooo tired! My doctor gave me a clue to this dilemma: commit to the time and the duration of the exercise, but modify the pace, the intensity. So I no longer strode along, full of energy. I strolled.

And while I continued to do the necessary things, I waited, not patiently, for the pain to subside.

I wanted to be rid of the pain. I wanted it to be truly gone, though, not merely hidden somewhere inside. In my impatience, I discovered another principle of redesigning my life: we can desensitize ourselves to things that might trigger emotional spells that are either badly timed or are unnecessary altogether.

I initially became aware of the importance of desensitizing myself when I went back to the symphony for the first time by myself. John and I had always so enjoyed this music together. In the familiar music hall, I was coming down a stairway into the lobby when a man crossed in front of me. I saw only his back, but his hair was white like John's and cut like his. He wore a sport coat almost identical to one of John's. My heart almost burst my rib cage and immediately immense disappointment halted my excitement. Adrenaline pumping, I closed my eyes against the tears. And I knew I didn't want to be surprised like this again. No more "first time back" surprises!

For me, that meant visiting all the places in our city that we had shared—the places we had lived, the restaurants we liked, the desert areas we picnicked in, the parks and museums and theaters where we had spent many lovely hours. These excursions were

> *We can desensitize ourselves to things that might trigger emotional spells that are either badly timed or are unnecessary altogether.*

hard. Sometimes I wept. Sometimes a simple poignancy arose in my heart. Sometimes tenderness melted my heart. But by making these jaunts when I felt strong, I took away that first-time shock when I confronted—without preparation—the reality of the change. Exposing myself deliberately to potentially painful memories strengthened me. I found life and love still in my heart in each of these places. God was in every one of them, as God always had been. Remarkably, John's love was still there, too. And my own loving as well.

Now I am free to go anywhere, because there are no more "first times back." When I realize now that I'm in a once-shared place, it gentles my soul. It feels good to be there—poignant sometimes still but deep-down good. I can feel the richness that our shared life left to my new single life.

With this desensitizing, I also felt that I had some power over the process of grief. I wasn't helpless. I could participate fully, in the way I chose for myself. I chose to redesign. Desensitizing myself was part of clearing the way for the new design to emerge.

Awareness of my power in the process carried over into the choosing and activating of new ways of being. This too is a principle of redesign: learn what nourishes you in your new life, pay attention to what you enjoy, and make sure you do it.

One of my exploratory activities was aimed at discovering what I could still enjoy, alone, that John and I had enjoyed together. For example, we had always liked long drives. So I found myself in the car a lot in those first weeks. I wanted to know if driving alone to watch the earth and the sky and the roadside wildlife could be enjoyable. Would this be a part of my new design? So I drove to favorite, familiar areas in Arizona, to campgrounds we'd visited, and I brought along food for myself and the birds. I took an overnight trip by myself. I went to a couple beautiful spots in the desert I had never visited before, exploring as we used to do together.

So, by doing, I learned that this, indeed, was a pattern that nourished me. I would keep it as part of my new design. In a similar way, I discovered that dining out alone, while I could do it without weeping, was not something I would keep. I would invite friends to go with me when I wanted a special meal.

I also learned that natural beauty of every kind strengthens and nourishes me. I spent hours and days wandering in the desert, under the warming sun. I sought open spaces and mountainsides, alone, soaking in the skies and the plants and the fresh air. I gazed long at flowers, almost tasting their color, their forms, feeling their delight in life. I went to a zoo and marveled at the animals. I got up in the night and let the stars astonish me. I watched sunrises and sunsets and moonrises and moonsets.

Art, always loved, now continued to feed me. I went to galleries and shops,

> *Learn what nourishes you in your new life, pay attention to what you enjoy, and make sure you do it.*

reveling in the creativity of so many people. I listened to music and let it wash my emotions. I went to plays and performances, sometimes with friends, sometimes alone. I always felt enriched by them so they stayed in my new design.

Beauty, whether in natural settings or in human creativity, is, I believe, an expression of God in the world. That's why it is so healing for us. Beauty touches our hearts and helps us stay open to life. Even in the easiest of times, haven't you felt the tears come when you see something exquisite? Doesn't music sometimes totally change your mood for the better? Although many of the ways I chose to redesign may be only personal, I believe that beauty in nature and art is nourishing to everyone. So I recommend that anyone who is redesigning spend time outdoors and in art galleries.

Another area I learned about is love and attachment. This one is subtler—and even more powerful than nature. I believe it, too, is universal and will help you. I experienced the difference between love and attachment in my spirit.

From almost the beginning of my exploration, I discovered that when I could be wholly in the present moment and feel only my immense love for John, there was always freedom, delight, pleasure. In the present moment, I knew that life is unspeakably wonderful. Love was sweet and set me free.

When my attention shifted to how much I missed him, wanted him back (even for a weekend!), felt the grief of separation—then there was pain, sorrow, bondage. This was attachment, rooted in what I wanted for me. Attachment, wanting, only intensified my pain. Yes, I knew I had to give these feelings their due, but knowing this difference between love and attachment freed my heart from ever believing that sorrow is the final truth. It isn't. Love is. Joy is. The grandeur of life in the present moment, in every present moment, is the truth. It is God.

Thus another principle became clear: the present moment is full of love, even delight; stay in it as much as possible. I practiced entering the present as often as I could remember. Perhaps my method will help you.

I would sit still, doing nothing. I noticed my body, how it felt against the chair, where I felt tired or lively, where I was tense. I let go of whatever tension I found. Then I attended to my surroundings, either in the house or out the window. I just looked, noticing how the light played or what little animals or birds I could see. Then I let myself enjoy this moment of quiet relaxation. I tuned in, inside, to love—perhaps thinking of John, perhaps of God, perhaps just being aware of love. And then it would happen: I would realize that the pain had slipped away.

> *The present moment is full of love, even delight; stay in it as much as possible.*

I was not able to remain long in this delicious state, but I was able to return to it often. What a comfort it was!

And God? Never absent. I was quite absent sometimes, but even in my absence from God, I never felt God had departed. I was just momentarily blinded in my heart by pain or wishing or weeping. Compassion, as profound as Christ, was there, waiting for me to return to awareness of it and receive. This truth enabled me to keep moving on the path of redesigning my life.

> *Compassion, as profound as Christ, was there, waiting for me to return to awareness of it and receive.*

Divine Compassion came again and again, startling me sometimes. It reassured me, it challenged me to get up and get going. It told me to like my life in its new parameters and to act on what the Spirit was urging me to do. It called me to pay attention inwardly more than ever before. Little by little I heard its basic message: everything you need, Marilyn, has been prepared for you. Do not worry. Just walk. Just let yourself love. Just open your heart and welcome every part of this most amazing experience.

Being open to all aspects of the experience of life after my spouse's death was not easy. Our life after such a death includes pain. That's it. How can we stay open to something so unwanted? I can't advise anyone else about this, because each person's response is so unique. What I knew for myself was that I didn't want this pain, which cost so much, to be wasted. I looked for ways to put it to work. When I relaxed with it, it would wash through me leaving me feeling better afterward. When I let it flow, it felt as if it were digging new channels in my being, which then could be filled with love and peacefulness. When pain seemed to overwhelm me, I put myself somewhere physically safe, like a bed, and let it do what it had to do. And always it subsided and left me open-hearted, even lighthearted.

A tentative tenderness about life would emerge in me that was sweet and kind. It was as if pain would sweep me clean to receive this gentle compassion. I wanted to keep this sweetness in my redesigned life. When I saw repeatedly that it came after a wave a pain, I resisted the pain less. So the new design came to include not only lifestyle changes but inner changes as well. All of them felt like gifts. I only had to welcome them, and I would receive them.

> *Just let yourself love. Just open your heart and welcome every part of this most amazing experience.*

Still, challenges continued. As each one arose, I would ask myself, *What can I do here that will support my new life, that fits into a single existence, that brings me enjoyment or love or friendship or pleasure or new awareness, that can teach me how to live now?*

One repeated challenge was, of course, holidays. It's common knowledge that these can be tough if you are grieving. John died in the fall, so the big family holidays were coming soon. What would help my redesigning? As I pondered what to do, I recalled that holidays come only once for the first time after a death. The first time would be the hardest. Those in the following years—well, I'd wait and see. But I wanted to be sure that the first holidays after John died were meaningful to me, that they contributed to my happiness at least as much as they brought awareness of the one who was not there.

And this is another principle: do meaningful things, do happy things. Support your own awareness of well-being, as you build your new life-design. If you do this, God will supplement your efforts with gifts you'd not design for yourself. Holidays will be no exception to this generous "policy" of the Lord's.

Looking ahead, Christmas was the scariest. I'd always loved Christmas. John and I had developed dear traditions, too. And they would feel empty now. I asked what I could do that would nourish my new way of life the most. If I had had children of my own, my answer might have been different, but I looked to the spiritual life I wanted to strengthen. How could I come closer to God? For years, I'd thought a Christmas retreat would be a wonderful experience. But I had always wanted to be with John and family, too. Now, however, I was asking myself, *What can I do with this holiday to rest more in God?* To that question the answer was clear: retreat.

So I went away for two-plus weeks over Christmas and New Year (leaving gifts prepared for all the family). During that time, I rested a lot and took in as much of the retreat as I had energy for. I also treated myself to a few extras: really good food, extra hours in bed, long walks in the coastal air. Taking care of myself was vital, so I protected my energy. It also made me feel good to know that I could do this for myself.

The greatest gift of the retreat, however, was an event I never could have designed for myself. My reader-friend, you may find this experience a bit strange. I assure you, I felt the same at first. But there is a reason I include it here, so please be patient with my story.

> *Do meaningful things, do happy things.*

For some weeks, I had been experiencing an inner pain that seemed to me to be too sharp for grief, somehow different from missing John. It felt as if I were being split inside with a sharp instrument! This pain came and went, but never having lost a spouse before, I didn't know whether it really was a part of the grief or not!

In a meditation course during the retreat, this pain returned at full strength. It interfered with my practicing what we were learning. So during a break, I spoke to the teacher about it. I asked her what I could do about this oddly sharp, recurrent pain that seemed so separate from the rest of my experience.

She looked at me—through me?—for a long moment, then said, "Part of your inner self has gone to be with John. You have to get it back."

The instant I heard her words, I knew they were accurate, even though I didn't fully understand. Part of me had slipped away. I could feel the split.

"How do I get it back?" I asked her. She suggested that I simply ask.

I went to my room. I lay on the bed, because I didn't know what was going to happen. I cried out inwardly to the Spirit and angels and saints and anybody else who could help. I begged them to come and do for me what I didn't know how to do.

In moments, I felt the Spirit's presence and someone else also standing alongside the bed. It was so strong, so clear, I could not doubt that help was being offered. I asked the Spirit to retrieve whatever was split away from me and bring it back to me. I waited. Little by little I became vaguely aware of what was missing in me. Nothing I could name and yet an important piece of myself—a part that I had never fully claimed.

Then I "heard" in my mind a question as clear as if it had been vocal. It was even a bit stern: "If I get it back for you, will you take care of it—finally?" My answer was immediate and certain, "Yes!"

Then I went into a state of no awareness. When I "came back" about an hour later, I was alone in the room. Half of my body felt different somehow.

For the next couple of weeks, I could actually feel that runaway piece at times—times when it seemed to want to slip away again. And I would say out loud, "No you don't! Come back here! You're mine!" Gradually, as the tendency to lose it lessened, so did my awareness of it as partly separate from myself. Even today I do not know in words what that piece was, but I do know that I feel more whole and more myself than ever in my life. I know without a doubt it began with that experience.

Since then, I have asked many people about this experience. I have learned that, although it is not much discussed, many people who lose a spouse do also seem to lose part of their own inner being. That gives rise to some of the immense pain for which we don't seem to have an explanation. Part of us tries to stay with our beloved, who now has no body. This is entirely natural. After all, when we are married a long time, our spouse holds a central place in our awareness, our activities, our choices. We are then a "we" and not only an "I." Some people become almost only a "we," and when that is broken, it is hard to rediscover the "I." It's easier then to let part of our psyche or our soul (who knows what this really is!) drift away to try to stay with the departed beloved. Just as re-claiming the whole "I" helps us redesign our life, so redesigning helps us become whole.

I have told my story in some detail, because it is far more common than we usually know. If you have felt split off from yourself by the death of your spouse, please turn to God and ask that whatever piece of you is lost be returned, so you can be whole.

This experience also taught me that when we ask urgently, even if we don't fully know what we're wanting, we will receive help.

Divine help, divine grace, is always available to us when we ask out of genuine need. We don't have to understand. We do have to be open to new experience, because when God is healing us, God may need to do something in us that hasn't happened before. If we shut

> *When we ask urgently, even if we don't fully know what we're wanting, we will receive help.*

that off either by not asking or by letting our beliefs dictate what God must do—well, God doesn't usually force a way past those attitudes.

Another recognition arose from this experience. The process of redesign will include not only the externals of living, like activities, but the interior of life as well—our attitudes, the qualities of our perceptions, the inner stance we take toward daily events. These are less easily accessed, it seems to me. I can decide to take a long drive and observe my responses. But in the more interior matters, I may not know what is needed or even what the choices are. For these, I had to trust God.

God, of course, always knows what we most truly need. God is also always willing to give us what we need for our next steps in growth. My question—Will this new "thing" support me in my new life?—had to be enhanced. It had to include my attitudes, habits of thought, even assumptions and what I always thought I knew about life. The experience of my inner split began to teach me all this. I hadn't known such an issue could even arise, much less what to do about it. Yet God led me to the right place and the right person, and God gave me the right healing.

Sometimes our attitudes are harder to let go than our habits of life. Here's a personal example again:

John was so loving that he was patient with my faults—so patient, he seldom mentioned them. After he died, my friends were not always so patient. They called me to account more than once for my habit of blunt speech, and that led me to examine what attitudes I held that allowed such speech. I really hadn't known that I needed to become more gentle inside. Had I only resisted the pain of grief, I might never have discovered my need for gentleness, either. But the pain forced a gentler attitude. Even then, had I not been alert to finding new ways of being now, I might have just pushed past this one and ignored the comments of my friends. As it was, they were supportive of new inner attitudes.

Each of us has inner issues. There are always inner situations, inner habits that need to be changed so that we can become whole. This process of redesigning our life can be extended to redesigning ourselves, with God's direction and strength. We need to be open to the possibility and willing to cooperate with the opportunities. They will come, because God wants us to be whole, so we can be love, so we can live in joy. If we want that, too, then openness to being taught inwardly is necessary.

> *The process of redesign will include not only the externals of living but the interior of life as well.*

All the experiences of my two years of redesigning (so far) have demonstrated beyond question that God's support is totally with me, aiding me to discover the helpful forms and needed qualities of this new phase of my life. I know that in our grief, God is "on our side." God wants to help us through this part of life, to use it to lift us into a renewed way of living, a fuller life, a life closer to God. And so, as odd as it seems in one way, I actually feel less alone than I ever have before. Gradually I have become stronger and more ready to take the next steps.

One of those next steps was another holiday—Valentine's Day. What to do? I would not get the Valentine I wanted that year, and I complained out loud to John that he might at least come to visit on that day. Yet I knew I would have to do something for myself.

Now I'd like to tell you that this time, too, I chose something high and spiritual. Nope! I sat in the home we had shared, now rearranged to suit me better, and looked around. I remembered something I'd wanted for some time, but I hadn't wanted to defend its cost to John. So up I got and out I went and bought it, a metal kitchen garbage can covered with flowers—red, orange, pink, purple, white, yellow, blue, with white pickets painted around the bottom. It made me grin. My Valentine to me.

Yes, it was poignant, but it was also quite grand, this garbage can.

It reminded me that aids to happiness come in many forms, little and big, spiritual and material. I must design into my new life elements of both. No longer would I put up with ugliness in my household just because of imagined money problems. I quit being stingy with myself, and the garbage can was my promise to myself to build more beautiful and engaging possessions into my newly designed life. I wanted to include the whimsical, whatever would make my eyes twinkle. This was my true Valentine to me—and it has lightened my life and heart.

The principle here? Do nice things for yourself just for fun. No, they won't be the same things that were fun before, but they will be a charming part of your new life-design, your new kind of happiness. Furthermore, just the freedom to do them, without asking anyone else, will strengthen you for living without a partner.

One of the nice things I had done earlier was to rearrange the contents of my home. Not everyone would find this helpful, but I did. One whole room had been dedicated to John's art, and it was full of paint, paintings, easel, frames, and other sundry equipment. I wanted to redesign that space so it was useful to me now, so it could be a space to support my own artistic interests. It meant changing a lot of other things in my home as well. It wasn't easy, because it broke a physical connection to my life with John. Yet to have a place where I could easily

> *Do nice things for yourself just for fun.*

make fabric wall hangings, where sewing machine and tools were ready, where a design wall could be built—what a lovely gift it was to me!

When the space was ready and I had begun to use it, I realized how necessary it would be for me to expand my love of making things, of creating, of designing and arranging. So I bought flowers and placed them on my prayer table in honor of love. I made for myself a quilt-throw to snuggle under and included patches from some of John's shirts. I continue to explore what creating means for me in my new life. What do I want to write? What do I want to make in fabric? And I'm signed up for a drawing class—a totally new idea, just for fun and to find out if I want to do that, too.

I believe this is another principle: exercise whatever creativity you have. It doesn't have to be formal or "artistic" or crafted. It may be arranging things—flowers, rocks, furniture, table settings. Arranging is also a creative expression. It could be cooking or making music or dancing or gardening or—well, you know where your own creative expression pleases you the most. Do this! It is so renewing. It affirms the richness of life. It draws us out of any stagnation we may experience when we are too tired or when we hurt.

> *Exercise whatever creativity you have.*

A friend of mine makes fountains. She doesn't give them away or sell them, because she likes to rearrange them and make new ones all the time. Every time one needs to be cleaned, it gets a totally new face. When she shows them to me, her whole being lights up. And she told me once that she likes to do one of these fountains when she feels a little down. It refreshes her being.

Creativity is very close to play. Play is not always too familiar to us as adults, but it is one of the changes that has occurred for me in the process of redesigning. It was taught to me in a most unexpected way, and from this event I learned that God is playful and full of wonderful surprises!

My birthday was coming up. Oh dear, what would that be like? I like birthdays, including my own. But now most people would probably not remember, and the celebration of life, happily shared with John, could be only imagined. I needed to do something special, different, true to the newer side of my life. I wanted to play, but how? I didn't know until the day arrived.

There seemed to be breezes that morning, so I dug into my closet and found the stunt kite I had bought a few years before. I went to a nearby park, put the kite together, and tried to get it airborne. The breezes seemed to stay far up in the trees, though. I stood the kite on its points, ran around, hollered at it, all to no avail.

Then I heard chuckling behind me. I turned. A shabbily dressed man was laughing at me. I couldn't blame him. He approached me very slowly, as if he didn't want to frighten me, and asked if I needed some help. I felt a bit uneasy, but my principles got the better of my nerves, and I said, "OK, let's see what we can do."

And suddenly the whole picture was hilarious—a sixty-one-year-old fresh widow and a dirty, probably homeless stranger, running hither and yon, trying together to get a kid's stunt kite into the air, laughing like a couple of idiots. The kite never did fly that morning, but the birthday surprise was tremendously life affirming. I'll never forget that unexpected celebration straight

> *God is playful and full of wonderful surprises!*

from God. Such celebrations await you, too. Look for them! Expect them! Be ready to welcome them!

I n my driving around Arizona, I allowed myself to follow all impulses to see where they would lead. That's a principle of redesigning, too. When you don't know what you want, you can explore impulses to find out whether they are true to your feeling for your new future or if they are just notions for the moment.

> *When you don't know what you want, you can explore impulses to find out.*

So as I explored places I'd previously visited and enjoyed, I allowed myself to play with the idea of moving there or even farther away, to a different state. Part of me seemed to like the idea of a big change, though I didn't know what form it would take or if it was only a notion. Thoughts of moving surprised me, because I had moved a lot in my life, and I was tired of doing that. I was quite happy where I was. Yet I had to give the idea attention, because I was still redesigning. As I pondered moving, I thought carefully about what I would be gaining. This reflection taught me something about what I valued. Then I'd think about what I'd be leaving behind. In this, too, I came to learn slowly what I valued. Aha! Another redesigning principle: take time to learn

> *Take time to learn what deeply matters to you, no matter how bizarre the search may seem.*

what deeply matters to you, no matter how bizarre the search may seem at the moment.

On one of my impulsive jaunts, I took along a friend who is a realtor. We began to talk about the advantages and disadvantages of owning my own home. So, since I was in the exploring mood, I agreed to let her show me some houses and talk about what I might want, if anything. And in this process I learned another principle of redesign: get clear about what you'd really like to have or where you'd really like to be, then see how close you can come realistically. "Realism" for me meant financial realism. To help myself toward clarity, I wrote a list of qualifications for my ideal house. When my friend showed me a house with nearly all of them, and within my price range, I was astonished indeed.

So I bought myself a house—first time ever. That has been a huge adventure! Moreover, I did not at all anticipate that it would give me a new feeling of stability. The house has become a tangible, visible base for the new life I have continued to design. Here in my new home, I am not faced daily with the absence of someone, but experience instead the presence of a new way of being in myself, in my own life—a life designed after my own pattern. Here I am free to create the environment I like best, which has turned into a sweet form of self-expression, another new experience for me.

> *Get clear about what you'd really like to have or where you'd really like to be, then see how close you can come realistically.*

All along the way, through all the newness and the challenge, the moments of delight and the moments of grief, I discovered that I could seldom maintain emotional clarity. Everything seemed ambiguous; I felt confused a lot of the time. Because both the pain of John's absence and the delights of new living were present, I couldn't sort them out. So I found that I didn't need to. Though it felt very odd to me, I allowed myself to move from one to another, giving each feeling its claim for space within my awareness. I learned that it's OK not to know how I feel or what I think, that it all may change tomorrow anyway. I learned to relax with emotional ambiguity. And since much of life includes ambiguities, this has turned out to be very useful.

> *Relax with emotional ambiguity.*

There was only one feeling that I absolutely refused to allow for more than a flash—self-pity. This is the most destructive feeling in all of life. It glues us to our selfishness. It keeps us from God. It prevents us from doing all the healthy and enjoyable and wonderful things that life offers us. It keeps us away from what and whom we love. And in grieving, it's a strong temptation, especially when our whole society defines death in terms of "loss" rather than "new life forms." So when "oh, poor me!" began to arise, it got short recognition and then a firm dismissal.

I would recall that the death rate on this planet is one hundred percent, that fifty percent of all married people go through what I'm going through, that it is part of life. I can't answer all the questions that arise around these facts, but I can refuse to feel sorry for myself for being part of the human situation. I can—and did—turn my attention resolutely to the beautiful and glorious in the human situation and in my own life. In doing so, I made sure my redesigned life would remain with me and not fade away into self-induced miseries.

In the months since John departed, a

great deal has changed in the externals of my life and also in the way I experience myself inside. I have learned so much about living! Some of it I've expressed in the principles in this book. Much of it is not so exalted. I've learned how to handle a drill and fix a leaky toilet tank; I've planted a lovely garden (first one ever) and wrenched my back digging in too-hard soil; I pay my own bills and clean my own coffee maker. My days revolve around new and different daily activities than they once did. As I continue to learn what my life means, what my purposes are, the questions I put to myself have also changed.

The biggest change of question is this: now I ask less frequently, "What do I want?" That has been important to discover, especially over the last two years of redesigning. But now I ask more often, "What is wanted of me?" What does the garden need from me? What does the house require of me? What do my friends need? What does my writing demand? And above all, what does God want of me? These questions teach me daily. They have removed some of the self-absorption that is part of grieving. It feels better to be looking, once again, beyond myself.

One answer to "What does God want of me?" seems to appear the most frequently: God wants me to receive divine gifts—"in spades," as we used to say. Now that the pain of grief has largely subsided, I can see that the past two years have brought gift after gift, grace after grace, endless generosity from God. Some of these gifts have been pure comfort, pure pleasure. Some have come wrapped in pain. But the most precious of all is one I thought I had invented myself—the decision to consciously redesign my life instead of letting grief determine my future. Now I know that even this was in fact a gift of God's love. And that's why I share it—because I know

> *Turn your attention resolutely to the beautiful and glorious in the human situation and in your own life.*

that if God wanted it for me, God wants it for everyone whose spouse has left the physical world.

Today I need no reminder to be grateful. Gratitude arises constantly, spontaneously, rich and full. It is gratitude for all that John and I had in those enchanted years together. It is gratitude for all I have now—renewed love for God, friends, new home, help when I need it, new lifestyle, opportunities opening on all sides. There is a strange and unexpected kind of security, too. It's as if the worst possible thing has happened and I'm still here, very much alive and full of joy, love, and a keen awareness of life's splendid invitation to adventure. I would not have believed it possible to be happier than I was in our married life, but I am.

And I'm no different from anyone else. Anyone can create, with God's help, a new life for themselves. And anyone can learn to be happy in a new way.

Best of all, little by little, the prayer of my heart that began soon after John died is being answered. I seldom think of John now without thinking of God. The loving I experience is more generic, more intense, and more God-oriented. Joy and peacefulness are their own sweet selves, available in my heart whenever I pause to look there. My choices, my actions, my prayers, more and more are simply offerings to the great loving God who sees all of us through everything with infinite imagination and creativity and compassion. This growing attitude of offering is the best of all this redesigning, and I didn't "do" that one! God lives in full compassion in every human heart, even mine, and that compassion has supported me and helped me grow through all the changes that have come after John's death.

We are so protected, so loved, if we just let ourselves be! In allowing, we discover that we can be all that we are, feel all that we feel, pray a lot, and go for God—no matter what has happened!

It's a new life.

It's a redesigned life.

Want to come?

Other Titles of Interest...

Coping When Your Spouse Dies
Medard Laz; Foreword by Emelia Alberico
This book helps readers realize that, while you can't bring back a spouse who has died, you can face your grief in a series of stages that lead toward personal healing.
ID #33610 • Paperback • $4.95

The Lord Is My Shepherd
A Psalm for the Grieving
Victor M. Parachin
Connects true-life experiences of grief and loss with central themes found in the Twenty-third Psalm.
ID #50600 • Paperback • $4.95

Death Is Only a Horizon
Thoughts in Time of Bereavement
A Redemptorist Pastoral Publication
Scripture verses, reflections, and quotations to soothe the bereavement process.
ID #34650 • Paperback • $2.95

Order from your local bookstore or write to:
Liguori Publications
One Liguori Drive, Liguori, MO 63057-9999
*Please add 15% to your total for shipping and handling
($3.50 minimum, $15 maximum).
For faster service, call toll-free 1-800-325-9521.
Please have your credit card handy.*